# The Theory of Cat Gravity

## (Being Robin's Pet Theory)

By Robin Wood

Decorated by Diana Harlan Stein

The Theory of Cat Gravity

A Livingtree Book / August 2000
createspace Edition

All rights reserved.

Copyright ©2000 by Robin Wood

Illustrations Copyright ©2000 by Diana Harlan Stein

ISBN:978-0-9652984-3-8

Book Design by Robin Wood

Cover ©2000 Robin Wood

For information, contact:

Robin Wood
3319 Greenfield Rd. #102
Dearborn, MI 48120

Or visit our website at:
robinwood.com

*Like all great scientific discoveries, more than one person has contributed to this theory.*

*The author would like to take this opportunity to thank all of those people.*

*Nancy, who first realized just what the cats were doing in those window ledges.*

*Tay, Jim and the Gang, who fleshed out a good deal of the rest one Friday at about 3am.*

*Barry, who discovered the completion of the theory early one Arisia morning, when he found out just how easy it was to get out of bed under certain circumstances.*

*And all of those people who listened to me while I Expounded the Theory at Science Fiction Conventions and Festivals across the country, and contributed pieces that I had not discovered.*

*A special Thank You to Diana Harlan Stein, whose delightful drawings grace these pages, and illustrate the theory. She took over the work of the art when I could no longer do it.*

*And a Very Special Thank You to my family, Michael and Skyia, who kept me fed and gave me massages not just while I worked on this, but on a daily basis.*

*To all of you, Thank you.*
*Without you, this book could never have been.*

This is the theory of Cat Gravity, which is my Pet Theory; and it goes like this.

Cats, as everyone knows, sit in the Window Ledges, where, as everyone knows, they collect Solar Rays. What everyone does not know is that they transform the Solar Rays directly into Gravity.

You can tell that they are doing this, because when they get into the window they hardly ever make any noise; and when they get out, they almost invariably go "thud."

Now, when a Cat is full of Gravity it finds a Person. If there are no people it will go to a Specific Chair, or a Specific Afghan; but they prefer people. And the Cat sits on the Person and pumps the Gravity directly into them. You can see them doing this, and you can hear them doing this, and this is why it is almost impossible to get up if there is a Cat on your lap, because you are having Gravity pumped right into your body.

If you are not the Actual Gravity Recipient you can easily lift the Cat off someone else's lap, and release them from the Gravity.* But if you are the Actual Gravity Recipient, you are more or less stuck until the Cat is finished, at which point it leaps lightly off your lap and has the Zooms all over your apartment.

*This proves that the immobilization has nothing to do with Not Wanting to Disturb the Cat. If that were the case, cats on other people's laps would also be sacrosanct, which is clearly not true. Also, people who live with cats often seem to take great delight in Disturbing the Cat, (probably because at some level everyone knows that it's All Their Fault,) and can frequently be seen Spinning the Cat, or forcing them to take part in Unnatural Acts, such as the famous Cat Dance.

You, on the other hand, are now so full of Gravity that you can barely manage to get up and stagger into your bedroom and lie down on your bed. Which you do, because, as everyone knows, you use more Gravity while you are horizontal than you do while you are vertical.

And while you are there, the extra Gravity leaks out of your body and into the bed. Which is why, when you walk past your bed, even if it is broad daylight and you are not particularly tired, you are likely to find yourself sprawled on it full length. The extra Gravity in the bed just sucks you right down, and there's nothing you can do about it.

Now, eventually the bed reaches what we call it's Gravity Saturation Potential*, at which point the extra gravity leaks out of the bed and lands on the floor, underneath the bed.

Which is why everything that's loose in the room winds up underneath your bed. There's just more Gravity there, and that's the way Gravity works.

*Gravity Saturation Potential is defined as the point at which an object cannot hold any more Gravity. Just where this point is depends on the density of the object. This is why waterbeds, which are very dense, can hold so much more Gravity (and consequently are harder to get out of) than conventional beds. This is also why the thinner your mattress, the easier it is to escape.

After a while, of course, the floor also reaches its Gravity Saturation Potential, at which point the extra Gravity seeps out of the floor and lands on whatever is below that. Which is why it is very important that you never set your house up so that your bed is directly above your dining room table.

Because, if you do, if you will end up with what we call a Gravity Enhanced Dining Room Table.

Gravity Enhanced Dining Room Tables are always covered with Stuff. Every piece of mail that comes into the house lands smack on the table, and there's not a thing that can be done about it. Most people who have Gravity Enhanced Dining Room Tables make no attempt to use them; they just take a plate and go to the couch. But if you have to use a Gravity Enhanced Dining Room Table, you will find yourself clearing a place by simply shoving things aside. There's no way to pick things up out of that Gravity Well; and even if you could, it wouldn't do any good, because something else would land there instantly.

Of course, sooner or later even the table reaches its Gravity Saturation Potential, at which point the extra Gravity oozes out of the table and lands on whatever is below that, eventually making its way into the basement.

Now, as everyone knows, basement floors are generally made out of Concrete. And, as everyone knows, Concrete is very dense. And, as everyone also knows, the denser something is the more Gravity it will hold. Therefore it would be reasonable to assume that basements hold a tremendous amount of Gravity, and this is in fact the case. This is why everything that's loose in the house eventually winds up in the basement, and once it's there it stays there. Getting something back up out of that Gravity Well is virtually impossible. When you move, you leave it there. The next people can deal with it.

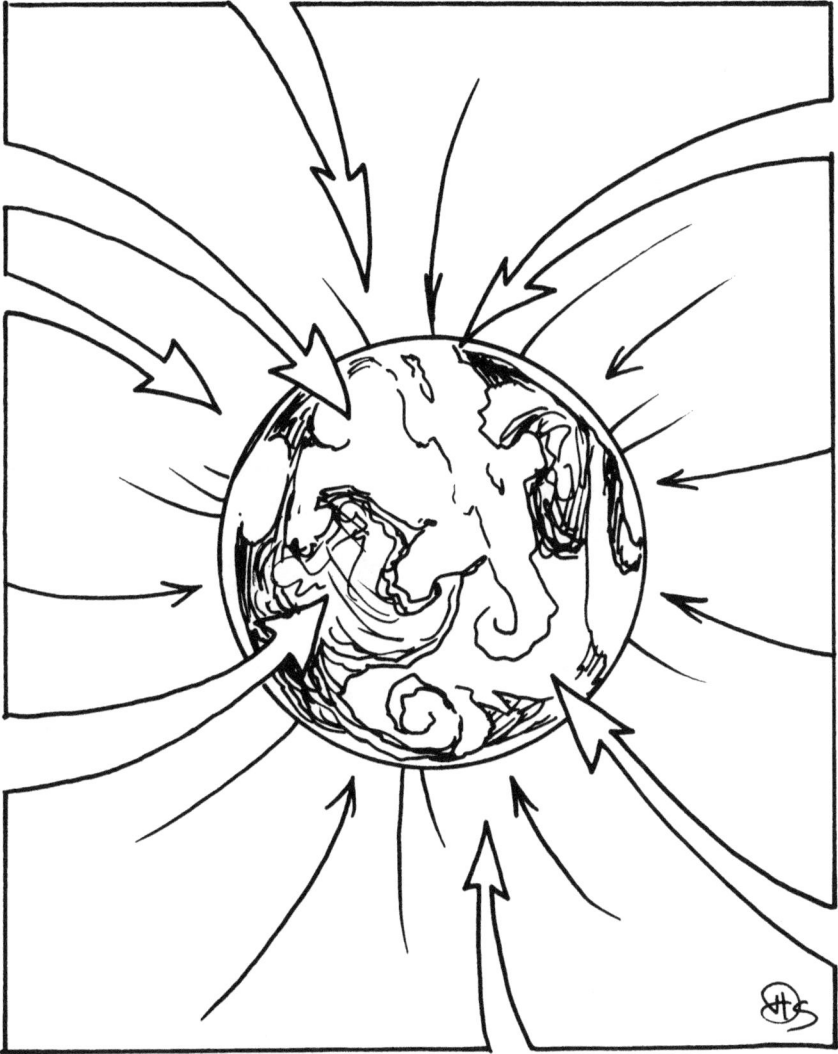

Ultimately, the basement floor also reaches its Gravity Saturation Potential, at which point the extra gravity falls onto whatever is below that, and so on, eventually working its way to the center of the earth, where it holds everything more tightly to the surface.

That is the basic Theory of Cat Gravity.

There are Proofs and Corollaries, and I will enumerate some of them here.(By the way, all of this is empirically provable in your own home with your own Cats.)

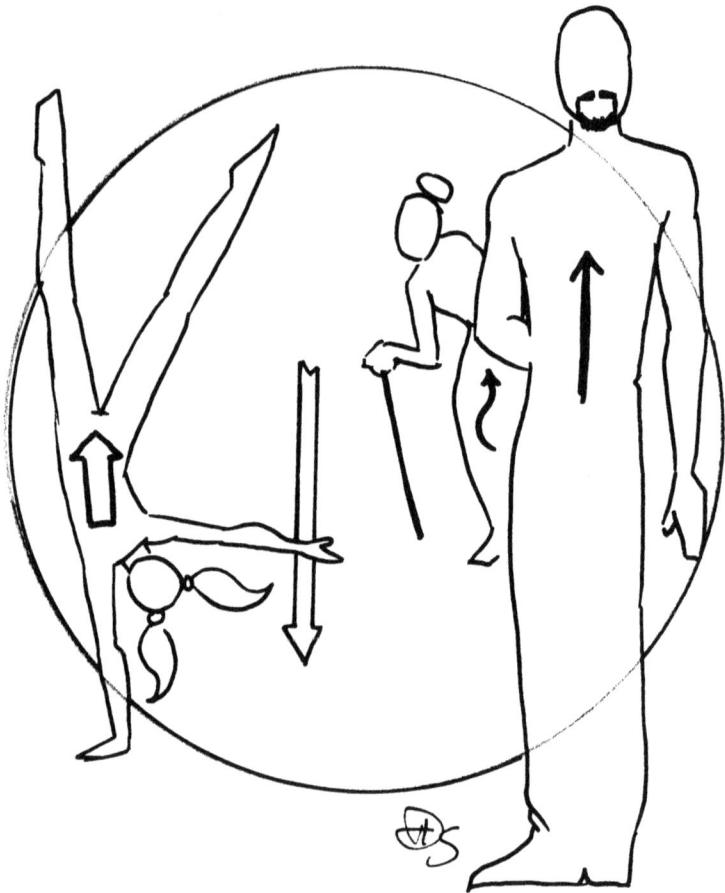

The First Proof is that, if this Theory is True, then there must be more Gravity now than there used to be, because the Cats have been busily making it for years.

And you know that's true, because when you were born, you are born into a certain Gravity Field, and you have no trouble with that Gravity. You can run, and jump, and climb onto chairs that are as high as your shoulders, and none of it is difficult.

The older you get, the more Gravity there is, and the more difficult it becomes to move.

By the time you're 40 looking up those stairs, it's a lot harder to get up them than it was when you were 10. By the time you're 90 they're probably pushing you around in a chair; and it's all because of the enormous amount of extra Gravity that's built up!

The Second Proof is that, if this Theory is True, Cats deprived of Sunlight will not have any Gravity unless they can get it somewhere else. And that, too, is clearly true.

Cats are far more active in the dark than they are while in the Window Ledge. And if there is no Sun, they can usually be found lying on a Bed, or a Gravity Enhanced Dining Room Table (or under it) or somewhere else that has a lot of Gravity built up. They can obviously reabsorb the Gravity, so they can use it to hold people down again.

The Third Proof is that, if this Theory is True, it should be easy to get up if a Cat with Little or No Gravity is on your lap. And that, too is clearly true! It would stand to reason that a Cat Without Gravity is far more restless than a Gravity Rich Cat, and the more restless a Cat is, the easier it is to simply shove it off your lap and go about your business.

As you may notice, that's Three Proofs. And, as Lewis Carroll pointed out many years ago, the proof is complete if only I've mentioned it thrice. And I have, so that Makes it True.

On to the Corollaries

My favorite Corollary is the Volume per Mass Corollary, which states that if you allow the Cats to sit on you Too Much, and you don't spend enough time in your bed to allow all that additional Gravity to leak out, you will be forced to add Volume to your body to hold the extra Mass the Cats have pumped into it. So, you see, it's All Their Fault! It's not the Häagen-Dazs® after all!

The Chair or Afghan Corollary states that if the Cat can't find a person (see the second clause of the Main Theory) it will deposit the Gravity into the Specific Chair or Specific Afghan. Which is why, if you try to sit on that chair, you will find it almost impossible to get up again because of all the extra Gravity in the Chair. And if you pull that Afghan over your legs because you get chilly watching TV, you are almost certain to fall asleep. All that extra Gravity on top of you is just too much, and knocks you out.

The next Corollary is the Dog Corollary. And it goes like this.

Cats are doing this on purpose, because they prefer people to be either actually feeding them, or lying down. And they know (because they have Sharp Claws and Really Pointed Feet) that they can always get people up to feed them. So they have devised a system to keep people lying down.

(Cat, by the way, is short for Catalyst.)

Dogs, on the other hand, would prefer for people to be active; either playing with them or taking them for walks.

When a Puppy realizes what the Cats are up too, which happens when it's about a year old, it concludes that its only hope is to use up as much Gravity as it possibly can.

Dogs do this by lying down, (because, as everyone knows, you use more gravity while you are Horizontal than you do while you are Vertical) and moving their tails very rapidly. When you see a dog just lying there with its tail going a mile a minute, what it's actually doing is using up Gravity at a ferocious pace!

This set of cross purposes explains why Cats and Dogs are such bitter enemies. (Unless, of course, they live in the same house. Then they can usually reach a compromise which often takes the form of the Cat playing with the Dog occasionally, and spending much of the rest of the time lying on it and pumping gravity directly into it. This reduces the Dog's desire to be active.)

The Sunless Day Corollary states that, if there is no Sun, then the Cats return to one of the other places where they have stored Gravity, such as the Bed, or Under the Bed, or the Chair, or the Gravity Enhanced Dining Room Table, or the Basement Floor. And they suck some of the Gravity back up so that they can transfer it into their people, rendering them incapable of anything except sitting down or lying perfectly still. Which, of course, is the whole point of the exercise. (This Corollary is used in the Second Proof, see above.)

The Not Having Cats Won't Save You Corollary concludes that not sharing your living space with Cats doesn't really make as much difference as you might hope.

You see, there are plenty of people who have more than one Cat. There are even people who have more than Ten or Twelve! And those people walk around in a Gravity Enhanced Condition all of the time.

They have so much Excess Gravity, in fact, that Gravity is percolating out of them everywhere they go. So they leave extra Gravity in every chair they sit on; in restaurants, or planes, or on the bus.

Then if someone with a Lower Gravity Field than the Chair now has sits there, Gravity is transferred from the Chair to the Person.

(It's complex, Thermodynamic stuff, and we don't need to go into that here.)

Suffice it to say that it has been observed that Gravity always leaches from a Higher Gravity Field into a Lower one, resulting in Gravity being transferred by something as simple as a handshake!

And then, of course, the person who doesn't live with Cats, but who now has Extra Gravity, goes home and lies down on their bed; and the whole Cycle begins.

The next Corollary is called Cats in Space. It concerns the effect of continually increasing Gravity on Relativity and the Movement of Planets. But the person who discovered it didn't write it down, and now it is lost.

And, finally, there is the Completion of the Theory.

As everyone knows, the opposite of Gravity is Levity.

And it turns out that Levity is held in Water.

This was discovered by my friend and associate Barry, who found one morning that in spite of the enormous amount of Gravity in his bed, when sufficient Water had collected in his body he was able to easily overcome the Gravity and make it into the bathroom.

He asserts that the Connection between Levity and Water is very clear. All you have to do is step on a wet patch on the sidewalk, and you will notice that the sudden lack of gravity causes that foot to slide away from the rest of your body.

As further proof, such slips are generally considered funny (at least by most Observers, if not by the Slippee.)

He also notes that the colder the water is, the more Levity it holds; which makes sense when you consider that Cats make gravity using Sunlight and Warmth. So Ice and Snow, which are full of cold, hold far more Levity than simple water. Which is why they are more slippery (and also more fun to play with.)

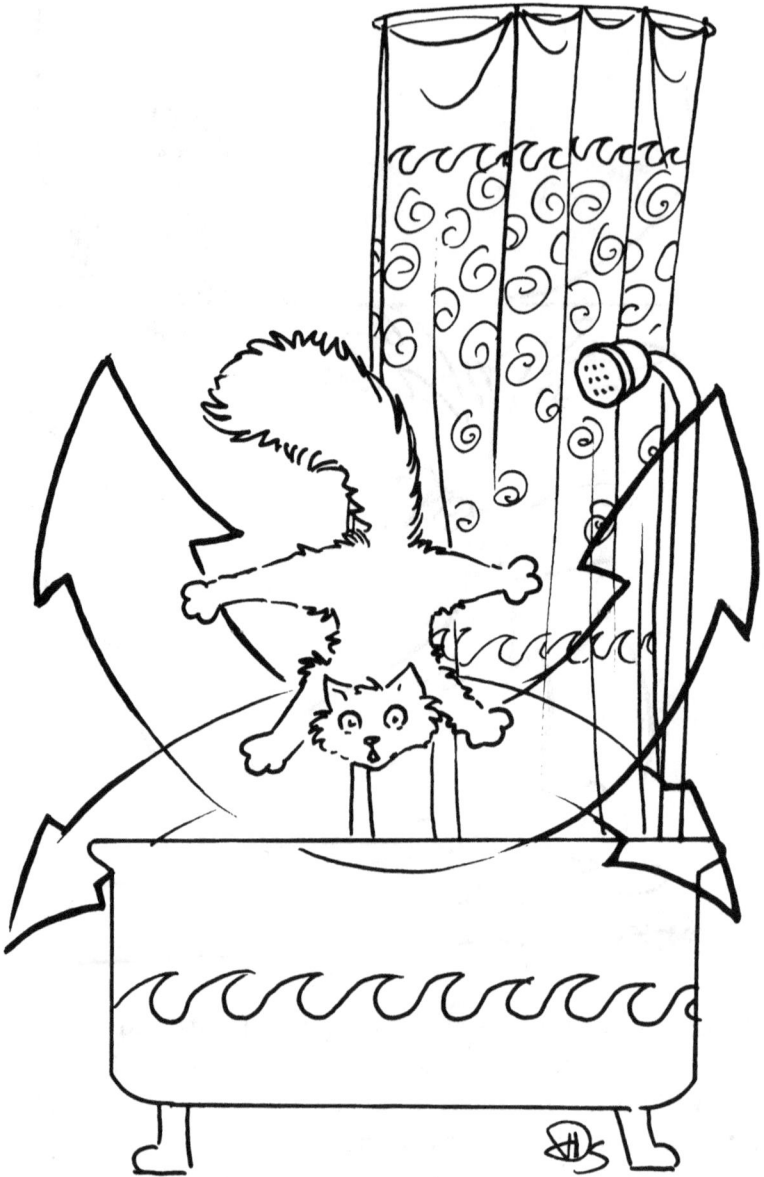

And Cats, those little Gravity Manufacturers, hate water.

If a warm, Gravity laden Cat accidentally falls into a tab full of water, you will notice that it bounces out without actually getting more than just its paws wet. This is because the Gravity and Levity repel each other.

Barry also found that sufficient Water can instantly remove all the Gravity from a Cat. You can prove the efficacy of this application of Levity by throwing water on a Cat and noting how very high the Cat springs into the air as its entire store of Gravity is released in a sudden burst.

Additionally, when water is thrown on a Gravity Rich Bed, the resulting reaction of Gravity vs Levity causes anyone lying on the bed to catapulted out and often to go flying halfway across the room.

As further proof, Barry points out that water releases the Gravity from Gravity Enhanced Dining Room Tables, enabling people to get things off of them with surprising alacrity. It is also the only thing that will reduce the Gravity Well of a Basement sufficiently to allow everything in it to be removed. If the basement floods, it's surprising how quickly it can be cleared of Stuff.

This explains why kids get so giddy around sprinklers.
And why it's so much fun to spend a day at the beach.
And why dogs love water.
And why dolphins smile all the time, because they live in the stuff.

That is the end of the theory to date; but as more research is being done, more things are being found out about Gravity (and Levity) all of the time.

Robin Wood's first feline companion was a tiny black kitten with green eyes. She was half Siamese, and half her-mother-got-out; and she came to live with Robin in 1981 in Okinawa, Japan.

She taught Robin many things, like how to move your hand really quickly, how to speak "cat," and how to play "fetch." She also taught her about Gravity, and how hard it is to get up when it's being Pumped Directly into your Body.

From discussions about this, and late night (well, okay, very early morning) sessions with her friends, the Theory of Cat Gravity was born. (See? You don't ever need to take drugs; fatigue poisons work quite as well, and are lots cheaper!)

Robin does lots of other things, too. Some of them are even semi-serious. If you want to see 'em, she has a website at robinwood.com.

And she sincerely hopes that you enjoy this book.


Diana Harlan Stein has been nominated for several Hugo Awards for Best Fan Artist. She has also lived with a bunch of cats, including Puddin', who was the most beautiful cat in the world.

She has a website, too, at naiadstudios.com